Daksha's Gourmet Spices
cookbookthree

Happy Cooking!

Daksha Narsing

www.**spicesgourmet**.com

Written by Daksha Narsing
Cover Design and layout by Amesh Narsing
Photographs by Tracey Kusiewicz

ISBN 0-9681253-3-6

APS Publishers
Distributed by
Daksha's Gourmet Spices
1050 11th Avenue
Williams Lake, B.C. Canada
V2G 3T9

Daksha's spices, cookbooks and cookware may be purchased at www.spicesgourmet.com or e-mail: daksha@telus.net

Printed in Canada by Friesens

To my Family

Bhaskar
Amesh
Pravin
Sarena

To the stars of my life for the peace,
Love and togetherness that we share
Now and forever.

Daksha

Preface

The inspiration for creating my vegetarian cookbook comes from my mother and grandmother who loved making delicious vegetarian dishes.

Creating these recipes has been a loving and fun-filled experience in my studio kitchen.

This vegetarian cookbook is created to compliment the spices we blend and sell at Daksha's Gourmet Spices, www.spicesgourmet.com. These recipes make it easy for anyone to prepare delicious vegetarian dishes.

Enjoy the flavors and aromas from my kitchen to yours.

Daksha Narsing

Acknowledgements

To my husband Bhaskar who is my partner both in life and business. Thanks for your input in ensuring that these recipes are perfect. Your everlasting love and inspiration mean everything to me.

To my children Amesh, Pravin and Sarena. Thank you for your continual support, encouragement and love. Amesh I truly appreciate the work you've done on the layout and design of this cookbook.

To my best friend and editor Shelly Peel for your patience and honesty. Last but not least to all my friends and students for encouraging me to create a vegetarian cookbook.

Daksha Narsing

The Origin

Vegetarian dishes are widely enjoyed throughout India not only because they are delicious but because of the health benefits.

This cuisine originates from the states of Rajestan and Gujarat, in India. My ancestry originates from Rajestan. The recipes and the blending of garam masala, thana jeeroo and chai (tea) masala have been traced back to Rajestan, going back several centuries.

I was born in Northern Rhodesia, Africa where my parents ran a business and raised six children. I have three older sisters and two younger brothers. At the age of eight I lived in India for two years with my sisters in a boarding school in Poona, India. During our school holidays in India, we would visit our grandparents in Gujarat. This is where I learned the value of the spices from my grandmother, who was the village herbalist and chiropractor. All of the villagers came to her for treatments for various ailments.

Later I returned to Africa, and learned my mother's style of cooking. I found it was similar to my grandmother's style as my mother had spent many years during her early married life with her mother-in-law. My mother taught me the importance of patiently picking, cleaning, grinding and storing spices.

My family then moved to England during troubled times in Zambia. I lived in England for seven years, until I met my husband Bhaskar and moved to Canada.

Celebrated spice combinations and recipes have been handed down in my family throughout the centuries, giving my mothers the knowledge they've shared with me. My cookbook is a culmination of my own recipes and those of my ancestors. I am delighted to share these wonderful recipes with you and your family.

How to Use This Book

This cookbook compliments the spices that are cleaned and blended by Daksha and Bhaskar Narsing of Daksha's Gourmet Spices. For best results buy spices directly from Bhaskar or Daksha via the internet at www.spicesgourmet.com or e-mail: daksha@telus.net. Our spices may also be purchased at retail outlets as shown on the website.

Throughout this cookbook many recipes call for fresh masalas. These are easy to make and can be conveniently stored in the freezer. To prepare ginger/garlic masala see page 74, green chillie masala see page 75 and garlic masala see page 76.

Refer to the Glossary section, starting on page 101, to fully understand Indian words and cooking vocabulary. Explore the Table of Contents and the Index provided in this cookbook to find mouth-watering recipes.

Try using our Meal Suggestions section beginning on page 97, but do not be afraid to put your own combinations of meals together.

Enjoy and Happy Cooking!

Daksha Narsing

Table of Contents

Table of Contents

Table of Contents

Appetizers

Moothya (Spicy Patties)

Ingredients:

2 cups cooked rice
1 medium grated potato
1 finely chopped onion
8 tablespoons chana flour
2 teaspoons ginger/garlic masala
½ teaspoon red chillie powder
1½ teaspoons thana jeeroo
1½ teaspoons salt
½ teaspoon turmeric powder
½ teaspoon baking powder
¼ cup water
6-8 tablespoons oil for frying

Method:

1. In a large bowl mix rice, grated potato*, chopped onion and chana flour.
2. Add ginger/garlic masala, red chillie powder, thana jeeroo, turmeric powder, baking powder and salt. Mix till crumbly.
3. Add just enough water until dough starts to bind.
4. Make 2 ½ inch round patties that are about ¼ to ½ inch thick.
5. Place patties in a heated frying pan with 4 tablespoons of oil on medium heat.
6. Cook patties on one side for 2-3 minutes. Turn patties over and cook for a further 2-3 minutes or till patties are golden brown. Add remaining oil, to cook with, as needed.

*Various types of vegetables can be used for example leftover corn, carrots, peas etc.

Paturi

Ingredients:

1 cup plain yogurt
1 cup chana flour
3 cups water
½ teaspoon red chillie powder
½ teaspoon turmeric powder
1½ teaspoons salt
1 tablespoon black mustard seeds
¼ cup oil
3 tablespoons chopped cilantro
3 tablespoons unsweetened shredded coconut
3 tablespoons sesame seeds

Method:

1. In a pan whisk together: yogurt, water, chana flour, red chillie powder, turmeric powder and salt. Allow to cook on medium heat stirring continuously, till mixture comes to a rolling boil.
2. Remove from stove once mixture is a thick consistency.
3. Spread a layer of mixture, approximately $1/8$ of an inch thick, over 2 or 3 greased or wax paper lined cookie sheets. Allow mixture to cool.
4. In a small pot heat oil on medium heat. Add black mustard seeds. Allow seeds to pop. Sprinkle oil and black mustard seed mixture on top of the paturi layer on trays.
5. Garnish with chopped cilantro, sesame seeds and coconut.
6. Lift one end of the paturi from each tray. Roll into swiss rolls.
7. Slice rolls into ½ inch to 1 inch slices and gently place them on a serving tray. Garnish with any left over chopped cilantro.

Paturis make a great snack and appetizer.

Patarya

Ingredients:

1 cup chana flour
½ cup corn flour
3 tablespoons rice flour
3 tablespoons all purpose flour
2 tablespoons ginger/garlic masala
1 teaspoon red chillie powder
1 teaspoon turmeric powder
2 teaspoons garam masala
2 teaspoons salt
2 teaspoons sugar
juice of ½ a lemon
6 tablespoons oil
¼ - ½ cup water
20 – 24 large sized spinach leaves (Swiss chard)

Method:

1. Wash and dry spinach leaves. Set aside.
2. In a bowl mix together chana flour, corn flour, rice flour and all purpose flour.
3. Add ginger/garlic masala, red chillie powder, garam masala, turmeric, salt, sugar, and lemon juice. Add just enough water to make a thick paste.
4. With your hand spread a thin layer of paste over one side of entire spinach leaf.
5. Take one side of leaf and fold to the spine of the leaf. Do the same with opposite side of leaf. Spread paste on folded parts of leaf.

Patarya cont.

6.　Roll spinach leaf, just like a cabbage roll. Set aside. Follow same procedure with remaining spinach leaves.

7.　Heat oil in frying pan on medium heat. Gently place pataryas in pan and cook for approximately 10-15 minutes, turning frequently. Ensure that pataryas are evenly cooked and are crispy on the outside.

Vadas

Ingredients:

¼ cup dokra mix (see page 24)
¼ cup cream of wheat
2 tablespoons corn flour
1 tablespoon rice flour
1 tablespoon all purpose flour
4-6 tablespoons plain yogurt
1 tablespoon sour cream
1½ teaspoons ginger/garlic masala
½ teaspoon red chillie powder
½ teaspoon turmeric powder
1 ½ teaspoons salt
½ teaspoon baking powder
2 tablespoons chopped cilantro
2 tablespoons sesame seeds
¼ cup warm water
4 cups oil for frying

Method:

1. In a large bowl combine dokra mix, cream of wheat, corn flour, rice flour and all purpose flour.
2. Add ginger/garlic masala, red chillie powder, turmeric powder, baking powder and salt. Mix well.
3. Add yogurt, sour cream, cilantro, sesame seeds and water. Blend together, making a thick mixture.
4. Heat oil in a wok or deep fryer on medium heat.
5. Drop small half inch balls of mixture in hot oil. Fry till vadas are crispy golden brown.

Vadas make a great party snack.

Bhajyas (Pakoras) see page 17

Bhajyas (Pakoras)

Ingredients:

1 cup chana flour
2 teaspoons ginger/garlic masala
1 teaspoon green chillie masala
½ teaspoon turmeric powder
1 teaspoon baking powder
1 teaspoon red chillie powder
2 teaspoons garam masala
2 teaspoons salt
5 tablespoons oil
1 – 2 cups water
1 cup finely chopped spinach
1 small potato grated
1 medium onion chopped
4 cups oil for frying

Method:

1. In a large bowl mix: chana flour, baking powder, oil, ginger/garlic masala, green chillie masala, red chillie powder, turmeric powder, garam masala and salt.
2. Add 1 cup water and stir. Add more water, a little at a time, until it reaches consistency of a thick cake mix.
3. Add grated potato, chopped spinach and chopped onions. Stir.
4. Heat oil in a wok or deep fryer on medium heat. Carefully drop about a tablespoon of mixture into heated oil.
5. Allow bhajyas to cook for about 2 – 3 minutes, turning occasionally. Remove bhajyas when crispy golden brown.

Serve bhajyas with tamarind chutney (page 70) or cilantro chutney (page 71).

Samosas

Vegetable Filling

Ingredients:

5-6 medium potatoes cubed
1 medium onion chopped
1 cup frozen peas washed and drained
2 teaspoons ginger/garlic masala
1 teaspoon green chillie masala
1 teaspoon red chillie powder
½ teaspoon turmeric powder
2 teaspoons thana jeeroo
2 teaspoons salt
1 teaspoon cumin seeds
6 tablespoons oil
4 tablespoons chopped cilantro (optional)

Method:

1. Heat oil in a pan. Add cumin seeds.
2. Add chopped onions. Sauté till onions are lightly browned.
3. Add diced potatoes, ginger/garlic masala, green chillie masala, thana jeeroo, red chillie powder, turmeric powder and salt. Stir well.
4. Cover and allow to cook on low heat for 15 – 20 minutes, stirring occasionally.
5. Add peas and cook for 10 - 15 minutes or till vegetables are thoroughly cooked.
6. Garnish with chopped cilantro and set aside to cool.

Samosa Pastry

Ingredients:

4 cups all purpose flour
1 teaspoon salt
4 tablespoons oil
2-3 cups water
½ cup extra flour for rolling out
½ cup extra oil to spread on pastries

Method:

1. Mix salt and 4 tablespoons oil into flour till crumbly. Add just enough water to bind dough. Knead dough to the consistency of a bread dough.
2. Take 1½ inch round balls of dough and roll out with a rolling pin or a velan. Makes 20 to 25 two inch flat pastry rounds.
3. Using a pastry brush, spread oil completely over the surface area of 2 inch round pastries. Sprinkle each round lightly with flour.
4. Join two, 2 inch pastry rounds together with oiled sides facing each other. Press the two together gently with your hand. These are now ready to roll again.
5. Flour both sides of double pastry rounds and roll out to about 6 - 8 inch round rotis.
6. Heat a tawa or flat frying pan on medium heat. Place roti on heated tawa and cook lightly for approximately 20 seconds. Turn roti over and cook on other side.
7. Remove roti and place on clean tea towel. Separate two rotis from each other at the point where they were joined before rolling. The rotis will separate easily.

Samosas cont.

8.   Cover rotis in a tea towel so that the rotis do not dry out.
9.   Once rotis are all made and piled on top of each other, cut them into 3 inch wide strips* with edges cut at an angle. This will give the pastry a trapezoid shape (see diagram on page 21).

*Keep the ends of the pastry and deep fry them until crispy golden brown. Sprinkle with salt and serve as a savory snack. Or sprinkle with cinnamon and sugar to serve as a sweet snack.

Samosas cont.

Diagram of how to cut the Roti

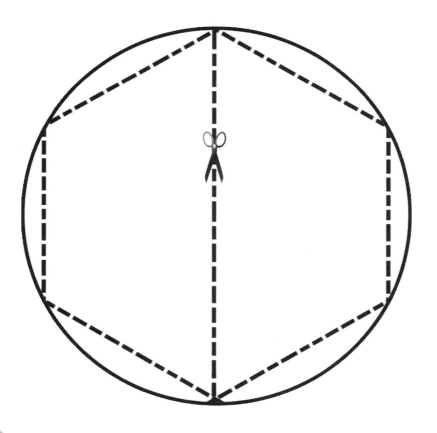

Cut along dotted lines.

Paste

Ingredients:

6 tablespoons all purpose flour
1 – 1½ cups warm water

Method:

Stir in enough water to make paste, the consistency of pancake dough. Using a blender, mix paste thoroughly till free of lumps.

Method of Folding, Filling, Storing and Cooking

1.   Brush paste on side A. Fold onto side B (see figure 1).
2.   Apply paste on top side of side A. Fold side C onto glued area, making sure side C hangs over leaving a ½ inch flap (see figure 2).
3.   Fill the samosa in the opening of the triangular pocket with approximately 1 to 1½ tablespoons filling. Brush paste on flap. Fold flap and seal Samosa (see figure 3), to make a triangular shape (see figure 4).
4.   At this point Samosas can be stored and sealed in freezer bags and frozen for later use.
5.   Deep fry Samosas in a wok or deep fryer on medium heat for 5 to 7 minutes or till Samosas are golden brown **OR** cook by brushing both sides of Samosa with oil or margarine (optional). Bake them on a non greased cookie sheet in preheated oven of 375°F for 8 to 10 minutes on each side or till golden brown.

Samosas make wonderful appetizers served with cilantro chutney (page 71) or tamarind chutney (page 70).

Figures showing folding samosas

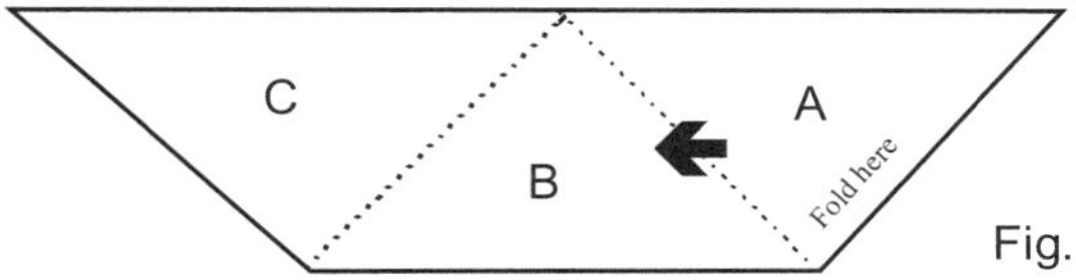

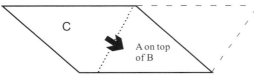

Fig. 1   Fold and paste flap A

Fig. 2   Fold and paste flap C

Fig. 3   Fill pocket with filling and paste

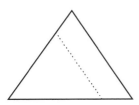

Fig. 4   A complete filled samosa

Dokra (Steamed Lentil Cake)

Dokra Flour Mix

Ingredients:

3 cups basmati rice
1½ cups chana daal
¾ cup urad daal

Method:

1. Sort through grains of rice, chana daal and urad daal, making sure there are no foreign objects.
2. Grind in coffee grinder, till mixture is a grainy powder.

Dokra (Steamed Lentil Cake) cont.

Ingredients:

3¾ cups Dokra flour mix (page 24)
500 g plain yogurt
2 teaspoons finely grated ginger
½ teaspoon green chillie masala
½ teaspoon red chillie powder
½ teaspoon turmeric powder
1½ teaspoons salt
½ teaspoon baking powder
1 cup warm water
2 tablespoons black mustard seeds
4 tablespoons shelled sesame seeds
4 tablespoons chopped cilantro
4 tablespoons unsweetened shredded coconut
4-6 tablespoons oil

Method:

1. Make dokra flour mix.
2. Combine together in a bowl: dokra mix, yogurt, green chillie masala, ginger, red chillie powder, turmeric powder, baking powder and salt.
3. Add warm water and stir well.
4. Let mixture stand covered, in a cool place, for approximately 4 – 6 hours.
5. Grease two 9 inch cake pans with oil.
6. Pour mixture into cake pans, filling them half full.
7. Sprinkle sesame seeds over top of mixture.
8. In a large saucepan heat about ¼ inch water.
9. Place 2 canning jar rings in water.

Dokra (Steamed Lentil Cake) cont.

10. Place 1 cake tray with mixture on top of rings, so cake tray is above water level and balancing on rings.

11. Cover and allow dokra to cook for approximately 30 minutes on medium heat, making sure water does not evaporate completely. If needed add more water down the side of pan keeping water level just under top of canning rings. To check that the dokra cakes are done, poke a knife through them. If it comes out clean, dokras are cooked.

12. Remove dokra tray from pot and allow to cool. Place another cake pan with dokra mixture in the saucepan ensuring there is enough water at the bottom of the pan at all times. Continue steam cooking dokra until mixture is used up.

13. Cut dokra into 2 inch squares while in tray. Do not remove squares at this point.

14. In a small saucepan heat 4 tablespoons of oil. Add black mustard seeds. Allow seeds to pop.

15. Sprinkle small amounts of oil and black mustard seed mixture over the cut dokra.

16. Garnish with chopped cilantro and shredded coconut.

17. Remove dokra from tray and place them in dish.

Makes approximately 4 - 6 trays of Dokras.

Serve with Traditional Chai (tea).

Spicy Vegetable Dishes

Paneer (Cheese)

Ingredients:

5 cups homogenized milk
juice of ½ a lemon

Method:

1.   In a large pot heat milk. Allow milk to come to a rolling boil.
2.   Add lemon juice slowly, stirring constantly. Milk will separate. Once this occurs remove pot from stove. Continue stirring till milk is completely separated.
3.   Allow mixture to cool for approximately 5 to 10 minutes. Then pour mixture into 4 layers of cheesecloth or clean cotton handkerchief. Gather edges and drain off as much water as possible.
4.   Open up cloth and spread cheese flat to about ½ inch thick. Cover cheese by folding cloth over.
5.   Place cloth with cheese on layers of kitchen towels and place a cutting board on top. Place weights on top of cutting board, e.g. mortar pestles etc.
6.   Allow cheese to sit for 1 hour. Remove weights and unfold cloth. Place block of cheese gently on a cutting board and cut into 1 inch cubes.
7.   Store in a sealed container in the refridgerator.

Paneer Bhaji

Ingredients:

4 cups chopped spinach
1 potato diced
½ onion chopped
1 tomato diced
1 teaspoon ginger/garlic masala
½ teaspoon green chillie masala
1 teaspoon cumin seeds
½ teaspoon thana jeeroo
½ teaspoon red chillie powder
1 teaspoon turmeric powder
1 teaspoon salt
4 to 6 tablespoons olive oil
1 cup paneer cubed (page 28)

Method:

1. Heat olive oil in pan on medium heat. Add cumin seeds and cubed paneer. Sauté. Allow paneer to turn golden brown. Remove from pan. Set aside.
2. Add onions and sauté. Add ginger/garlic masala, green chillie masala, thana jeeroo, red chillie powder, turmeric powder and salt. Stir.
3. Add spinach and potatoes. Stir. Cook covered for 5 to 10 minutes, stirring occasionally.
4. Add sautéd paneer. Allow to cook for 5 to 10 minutes, stirring occasionally or till spinach and potatoes are cooked.
5. Add tomatoes and allow to cook for 5 to 10 minutes.
6. Serve Paneer Bhaji with roti or naan bread.

Aloo Gobi (Cauliflower Potato Curry)

Ingredients:

2 cups chopped cauliflower
1 onion chopped
2 tomatoes diced
2 potatoes diced
1 cup frozen peas
1 teaspoon cumin seeds
1 teaspoon black mustard seeds
2 teaspoons ginger/garlic masala
½ teaspoon green chillie masala
2 teaspoons thana jeeroo
1 teaspoon red chillie powder
½ teaspoon turmeric powder
1½ teaspoons salt
4 tablespoons oil
2 tablespoons chopped cilantro (optional)

Method:

1. Heat oil in pan. Add cumin seeds and black mustard seeds. Allow seeds to sizzle and pop.
2. Add onions immediately and sauté.
3. Add cauliflower and potatoes to onions. Stir.
4. Add ginger/garlic masala, green chillie masala, thana jeeroo, red chillie powder, turmeric powder and salt. Stir.
5. Cover and allow to cook on medium heat for 10 minutes, stirring occasionally.
6. Add frozen peas and allow to cook for a further 5 minutes.
7. Add tomatoes and cook on low heat, stirring occasionally, for another 5 to 10 minutes, or till vegetables are thoroughly cooked.
8. Garnish with chopped cilantro.

Spinach Curry

Ingredients:

8 cups chopped spinach
1 onion chopped
2 tomatoes diced
2 potatoes cut into ½ inch cubes
2 teaspoons cumin seeds
2 teaspoons ginger/garlic masala
¼ teaspoon green chillie masala
1½ teaspoons thana jeeroo
1 teaspoon red chillie powder
½ teaspoon turmeric powder
1½ teaspoons salt
6 tablespoons oil

Method:

1. Heat oil in pan on medium heat. Add cumin seeds. Allow the seeds to sauté and brown slightly.
2. Add chopped onions and sauté.
3. Add ginger/garlic masala, green chillie masala, thana jeeroo, red chillie powder, turmeric powder and salt. Stir well.
4. Add cubed potatoes and stir. Cook covered for 5 minutes.
5. Add chopped spinach. Cover and allow to cook for 15 minutes, stirring occasionally.
6. Add diced tomatoes. Allow to cook for another 10 – 15 minutes on low heat, or till vegetables are thoroughly cooked.

Karela

Ingredients:

2 cups brine – dissolve 2 teaspoons of salt in 2 cups of water
2 cups thinly sliced karela
1 finely chopped onion
2 tomatoes diced
1 teaspoon cumin seeds
1½ teaspoons ginger/garlic masala
½ teaspoon green chillie masala
1 ½ teaspoons thana jeeroo
½ teaspoon red chillie powder
1 teaspoon turmeric powder
1½ teaspoons salt
6 tablespoons oil
2 tablespoons chopped cilantro (optional)

Method:

1. Soak karela in a dish with 2 cups brine for 2 hours. Drain.
2. Heat oil in frying pan on medium heat. Add cumin seeds. Allow cumin seeds to brown slightly.
3. Add chopped onions and sauté.
4. Add drained karela, ginger/garlic masala, green chillie masala, red chillie powder, turmeric powder and salt. Stir.
5. Cover and cook on medium heat for 10 to 15 minutes, stirring occasionally.
6. Add diced tomatoes and cover. Cook for a further 10 to 15 minutes, stirring occasionally or till both karela and tomatoes are cooked and slightly browned.
7. Garnish with freshly chopped cilantro.

Okra Curry see page 34

Eggplant Potato Curry see page 33

Eggplant Potato Curry

Ingredients:

1 large eggplant
1 potato diced
1 onion chopped finely
2 tomatoes diced
1 teaspoon ginger/garlic masala
½ teaspoon green chillie masala
1 teaspoon thana jeeroo
½ teaspoon red chillie powder
½ teaspoon turmeric powder
1 teaspoon cumin seeds
1 teaspoon salt
4 tablespoons oil
1 tablespoon chopped cilantro (optional)

Method:

1. Heat oil in a pan, on medium heat. Add cumin seeds and onions. Sauté
2. Cut eggplant into small 1 inch cubes. Peel and dice potatoes to ½ inch cubes.
3. Add potato and eggplant to pan and stir.
4. Add ginger/garlic masala, green chillie masala, thana jeeroo, red chillie powder, turmeric powder and salt. Stir. Allow to cook covered on low heat for 15 – 20 minutes stirring occasionally.
5. Add diced tomatoes and allow to cook for another 10 minutes or till vegetables are cooked.
6. Garnish with chopped cilantro.

Okra Curry

Ingredients:

2 cups thinly sliced okra
1 finely chopped onion
2 tomatoes diced
1 teaspoon cumin seeds
1½ teaspoons ginger/garlic masala
½ teaspoon green chillie masala
1 ½ teaspoons thana jeeroo
½ teaspoon red chillie powder
1 teaspoon turmeric powder
1½ teaspoons salt
6 tablespoons oil
2 tablespoons chopped cilantro (optional)

Method:

1. Heat oil in a frying pan on medium heat. Add cumin seeds. Allow cumin seeds to brown slightly.
2. Add onions and sauté.
3. Add okra, ginger/garlic masala, green chillie masala, thana jeeroo, red chillie powder, turmeric powder and salt. Stir.
4. Cover and cook on medium heat for 10 to 15 minutes, stirring occasionally.
5. Add tomatoes and cover. Cook for 10 to 15 minutes, stirring occasionally or till both okra and tomatoes are cooked and slightly browned.
6. Garnish with freshly chopped cilantro.

Raveya (Stuffed Eggplant)

Ingredients:

6 small eggplants
1 finely chopped onion
3 tablespoons crushed unsalted peanuts
2 tablespoons chopped cilantro
1 ½ teaspoons ginger/garlic masala
½ teaspoon green chillie masala
1 ½ teaspoons thana jeeroo
½ teaspoon red chillie powder
½ teaspoon turmeric powder
1 ½ teaspoons salt
4 tablespoons oil

Method:

1. Make crumbly filling by mixing: chopped onions, crushed peanuts, ginger/garlic masala, green chillie masala, thana jeeroo, red chillie powder, turmeric powder, salt and chopped cilantro.
2. Wash eggplants and cut off tops. Scoop out half of the eggplant. Set aside.
3. Fill each eggplant with stuffing, making sure stuffing is all the way to the bottom.
4. In a pan heat oil on low heat. Gently place stuffed eggplants in pan.
5. Cover and allow to cook on low heat for 20 – 25 minutes or till eggplants are thoroughly cooked.

Vegetable Pilaf

Ingredients:

2 cups basmati rice
2 teaspoons salt
4 cups water

Method:

1. Wash basmati rice 3 times. Put in pot with water and salt.
2. Allow rice to cook on medium heat for about 10 to 15 minutes or till rice is half cooked.
3. Remove from stove and drain off water in a sieve. Set aside.

Vegetable Pilaf cont.

Ingredients:

2 medium potatoes diced
2 carrots chopped
1 cup green beans chopped
1 cup whole sweet peas
1 cup frozen peas
1 onion sliced
2 teaspoons ginger/garlic masala
1 teaspoon green chillie masala
2 teaspoons thana jeeroo
1 teaspoon red chillie powder
½ teaspoon turmeric powder
1 teaspoon cumin seeds
1½ teaspoons salt
1 tablespoon sesame seeds
½ cup water
4 tablespoons oil
2 tablespoons chopped cilantro (optional)
Half cooked basmati rice (page 36)

Method:

1.   Heat oil in a large pot. Add cumin seeds and sliced onions. Sauté.
2.   Add diced potatoes, carrots, green beans, sweet peas and frozen peas. Stir in ginger/garlic masala, green chillie masala, thana jeeroo, red chillie powder, turmeric powder and salt.
3.   Cover and cook on medium heat for 10 minutes, stirring vegetables occasionally.
4.   Spread half cooked basmati rice over top of vegetables. Add water. Cover and cook pilaf on low heat for 15 to 20 minutes or till rice and vegetables are thoroughly cooked.
5.   Serve on large platter and garnish with sesame seeds and chopped cilantro.

Vegetable Stir Fry

Ingredients:

½ green pepper julienned
½ red pepper julienned
2 carrots julienned
½ cup cauliflower chunks
1 cup whole sweet peas or snow peas
1 red onion sliced
¼ cup green onions chopped
2 teaspoons ginger/garlic masala
½ teaspoon green chillie masala
2 garlic cloves thinly sliced
2 teaspoons thana jeeroo
½ teaspoon red chillie powder
½ teaspoon turmeric powder
1½ teaspoons salt
4 tablespoons oil
1 tablespoon chopped cilantro (optional)
1 tablespoon chopped parsley (optional)

Method:

1. In a pan heat oil on medium heat. Add thinly sliced garlic, ginger/garlic masala and green chillie masala. Stir.
2. Add thinly sliced red onions and green onions. Sauté.
3. Add green peppers, red peppers, carrots, cauliflower and whole sweet peas. Stir.
4. Add thana jeeroo, red chillie powder, turmeric powder and salt. Stir.
5. Allow to cook for 10 to 15 minutes on medium heat, stirring occasionally. If you prefer crunchy vegetables shorten the cooking time.
6. Garnish with chopped cilantro and parsley.

Daals & Beans

Bhakro

Ingredients:

3¾ cups Dokra flour mix (page 24)
500 g plain yogurt
1 medium onion sliced
2 cups finely chopped spinach
2 teaspoons ginger/garlic masala
1 teaspoon green chillie masala
½ teaspoon red chillie powder
1 teaspoon turmeric powder
1 teaspoon baking powder
2 teaspoons salt
1 cup warm water
6 tablespoons oil
1 tablespoon black mustard seeds
4 tablespoons sesame seeds
2 tablespoons chopped cilantro (optional)

Method:

1. In a bowl combine: dokra mix, yogurt, warm water, ginger/garlic masala, green chillie masala, red chillie powder, turmeric powder, baking powder and salt.
2. Let mixture stand covered in a cool place for 2 to 4 hours.
3. Stir into mixture onions and spinach.
4. Pour mixture into a greased pan 13" x 9". Sprinkle with sesame seeds.
5. Bake in a preheated oven at 375°F for 40 to 45 minutes.
6. Remove pan from oven and cut into 2 inch squares. Do not remove from pan at this point.
7. In a small saucepan heat 6 tablespoons of oil. Add black mustard seeds and allow to pop.

Bhakro cont.

8.   Sprinkle small amounts of oil and black mustard seed mixture over baked Bhakro.
9.   Garnish with chopped cilantro.
10.   Remove Bhakro from cake pan and place on a platter.

Chevtee Daal

Ingredients:

1 cup toower daal
1 cup urad daal
1½ teaspoons ginger/garlic masala
½ teaspoon green chillie masala
1½ teaspoons garam masala
½ teaspoon red chillie powder
½ teaspoon turmeric powder
1 teaspoon salt
4 tablespoons ghee or butter
3 – 4 cups water

Method:

1. Wash and rinse toower daal and urad daal.
2. Place both daals in a pressure cooker. Cook with 3 cups water (or cook covered in deep pan with 4 cups of water, on medium heat). Cook daal thoroughly.
3. Strain daal through a fine sieve into a dish.
4. Add red chillie powder, turmeric powder, one teaspoon garam masala and salt. Stir well
5. In a pot melt ghee or butter on medium heat. Add ginger/garlic masala and green chillie masala. Sauté.
6. Add daal and stir. Cover and allow the daal to come to a boil, stirring constantly. Daal is now cooked.
7. Sprinkle half a teaspoon garam masala over daal to garnish.

3 Bean Vadhu (Sprouted Bean Curry)

Ingredients:

½ cup green mung beans
½ cup brown mung beans
½ cup black mung beans
1½ onions thinly sliced
1½ teaspoons ginger/garlic masala
¾ teaspoon green chillie masala
1 teaspoon thana jeeroo
½ teaspoon red chillie powder
½ teaspoon turmeric powder
1 teaspoon salt
½ - ¾ cup water
6 tablespoons oil

Method:

1.　　Soak green, brown and black mung beans in warm water in a large bowl (with one inch water above level of beans). Soak for approximately 3 hours or till beans increase to twice the size.
2.　　Drain and tie beans in a clean cheesecloth or kitchen towel. Place bundle of beans in a deep dish and store in a dark place for 12 to 16 hours or till beans have sprouted.
3.　　Remove sprouted beans from cloth. Wash beans gently trying not to break sprouts. Drain in a colander.
4.　　In a large saucepan heat oil on medium heat. Add onions and sauté.
5.　　Add sprouted beans, ginger/garlic masala, green chillie masala, thana jeeroo, red chillie powder, turmeric powder and salt. Stir well.
6.　　Cook on low heat covered for approximately 40 to 60 minutes stirring occasionally or till beans are thoroughly cooked.

Mung Daal Soup

Ingredients:

2 cups mung daal
1½ teaspoons ginger/garlic masala
½ teaspoon green chillie masala
½ teaspoon red chillie powder
½ teaspoon turmeric powder
1 teaspoon salt
4 pieces cassia sticks
3 whole cloves
4 tablespoons ghee or butter
2 tablespoons chopped cilantro (optional)
3 - 4 cups water

Method:

1. Wash mung daal. Cook on medium heat in a large saucepan with 3 to 4 cups water. Cook for approximately 30 to 40 minutes till daal is thoroughly cooked.
2. Strain daal through a fine sieve into a dish.
3. Add ginger/garlic masala, green chillie masala, red chillie powder, turmeric powder and salt. Stir well.
4. In a saucepan melt ghee on medium heat. Add cassia sticks and cloves.
5. Add sieved daal and stir. Cover and allow daal to come to a boil, stirring constantly.
6. Garnish with chopped cilantro.

Spicy Black Eye Beans

Ingredients:

1 cup black eye beans
½ onion diced
1 tomato diced
1 teaspoon ginger/garlic masala
1 teaspoon thana jeeroo
½ teaspoon red chillie powder
¼ teaspoon turmeric powder
1 teaspoon sweet basil
½ teaspoon oregano
1 teaspoon salt
2 tablespoons tomato paste
1 tablespoon brown sugar
2 teaspoons white wine vinegar
10 – 12 ajwan seeds
4 tablespoons oil
¼ cup water

Method:

1. Cook beans in plenty of water on medium heat for 20 to 30 minutes or till beans are fully cooked.
2. Drain beans and place in a deep dish. Add ginger/garlic masala, thana jeeroo, red chillie powder, turmeric powder and salt.
3. Heat oil in a saucepan on medium heat. Add ajwan seeds and chopped onions. Sauté.
4. Add beans and stir. Add diced tomatoes, tomato paste, water, vinegar, sweet basil and oregano. Stir well.
5. Add brown sugar and stir. Allow to cook for 20 to 30 minutes on low heat.

Serve with plain yogurt and naan bread or roti.

Tangy Mung Bean Curry

Ingredients:

1½ cups green mung beans
1 tomato chopped
1¼ teaspoons ginger/garlic masala
½ teaspoon green chillie masala
¼ teaspoon red chillie powder
½ teaspoon turmeric powder
½ teaspoon black mustard seeds
juice of half a lemon
½ cup water
4 curry leaves (limeree leaves)
1½ teaspoons salt
4 tablespoons oil
1 tablespoon chopped cilantro (optional)

Method:

1. Wash mung beans and cook on medium heat in a deep saucepan with about 4 cups of water. Add chopped tomato and allow to cook for 30 to 40 minutes (Beans will split open when cooked).
2. In a separate saucepan heat oil on medium heat. Add black mustard seeds and limeree leaves.
3. Add cooked mung beans, ginger/garlic masala, green chillie masala, red chillie powder, turmeric powder, lemon juice, ½ cup water and salt. Stir well.
4. Allow mung to cook for 10 to 15 minutes, stirring occasionally.
5. Garnish with chopped cilantro.

Serve over a bed of basmati rice with plain yogurt on the side.

Curried Bean Medley

Ingredients:

1 - 19 fl oz can mixed beans
½ onion chopped
1 tomato diced
2 teaspoons ginger/garlic masala
¼ teaspoon green chillie masala
1½ teaspoons thana jeeroo
½ teaspoon red chillie powder
½ teaspoon turmeric powder
1 teaspoon cumin seeds
1¼ teaspoons salt
¼ - ½ cup water
4 tablespoons oil
1 tablespoon chopped cilantro (optional)

Method:

1. Heat oil in a pan on medium heat. Add cumin seeds.
2. Add chopped onions. Sauté.
3. Wash and drain mixed beans. Add to onions and stir.
4. Add ginger/garlic masala, green chillie masala, thana jeeroo, red chillie powder, turmeric powder and salt. Stir well.
5. Add water and cook covered for 10 to 15 minutes.
6. Add diced tomatoes and stir. Cook for a further 10 to 15 minutes stirring occasionally.
7. Garnish with chopped cilantro.

Kadhee

Ingredients:

½ cup chana flour
1 litre buttermilk
2 teaspoons garlic masala
½ teaspoon green chillie masala
½ teaspoon red chillie powder
½ teaspoon turmeric powder
2 teaspoons cumin seeds
1½ teaspoons salt
6 limeree leaves (curry leaves)
2 tablespoons ghee
2 cups water
1 tablespoon chopped cilantro (optional)

Method:

1. In a large bowl whisk together chana flour and buttermilk.
2. Stir in garlic masala, green chillie masala, red chillie powder, turmeric powder and salt.
3. In a deep saucepan melt ghee on medium heat. Add limeree leaves and cumin seeds. Allow seeds to sizzle.
4. Add buttermilk mixture and cover immediately. Keep covered for one minute to capture flavors.
5. Add water and stir constantly till Kadhee comes to a full rolling boil.
6. Sprinkle with chopped cilantro.

Serve over a bed of basmati rice or vegetable pilaf.

Chana Masala see page 49

Chana Masala

Ingredients:

1 - 19 fl oz can chick peas
½ onion chopped
½ green pepper diced
2 teaspoons ginger/garlic masala
1 teaspoon thana jeeroo
½ teaspoon garam masala
1 teaspoon red chillie powder
½ teaspoon turmeric powder
1¼ teaspoons salt
1 teaspoon cumin seeds
1 tablespoon brown sugar
½ cup crushed tomatoes
4 tablespoons oil

Method:

1. Heat oil in a pan on medium heat. Add cumin seeds. Allow seeds to sizzle.
2. Add chopped onions and sauté.
3. Add diced green peppers and stir.
4. Add washed and drained chick peas. Stir.
5. Add ginger/garlic masala, thana jeeroo, garam masala, red chillie powder, turmeric powder and salt. Stir.
6. Cook covered for 10 – 15 minutes, stirring occasionally.
7. Add crushed tomato and brown sugar. Allow to cook for 5 – 10 minutes on low heat.

If you want this dish more soupy, add another ½ cup crushed tomatoes and ¼ cup water.

Toower Daal

Step I

Ingredients:

1 cup toower daal
1 tomato chopped
¼ teaspoon red chillie powder
¼ teaspoon turmeric powder
¼ teaspoon salt
3 – 4 cups water

Method:

1. Wash daal thoroughly in warm water.
2. In a large saucepan add daal, red chillie powder, turmeric powder, salt and water.
3. Add large chunks of tomato. Cook daal covered on medium heat in a saucepan for 20 to 30 minutes or till daal is cooked to a pulp. (To speed up the process cook daal in a pressure cooker for 10 to 15 minutes).
4. Sieve daal into a large bowl and set aside.

Toower Daal cont.

Step II

Ingredients:

3 teaspoons grated ginger
¾ teaspoon red chillie powder
½ teaspoon turmeric powder
1 teaspoon salt
3 whole dry red chillies
1 teaspoon black mustard seeds
1 teaspoon cumin seeds
1½ tablespoons brown sugar
juice of one lemon
4 tablespoons oil
½ - 1 cup water
1 tablespoon chopped cilantro (optional)

Method:

1. Add to sieved daal: grated ginger, red chillie powder, turmeric powder, juice of one lemon and salt. Stir well.
2. Add water (if you prefer a thick consistency add less water). Stir.
3. Heat oil in a separate pan on medium heat. Add whole dry red chillies, black mustard seeds and cumin seeds.
4. Immediately add daal and cover quickly to trap flavors in daal.
5. Cook till daal comes to a rolling boil.
6. Add brown sugar and allow to cook for 5 minutes on low heat.
7. Garnish with chopped cilantro.

Notes

Snacks, Breads & Rice Dishes

Flaky Roti (Chapatti)

Ingredients:

1 cup all purpose flour
1 cup whole wheat flour
2 tablespoons oil
1 teaspoon salt
1 – 2 cups hot water
½ cup all purpose flour
¼ cup oil

Method:

1.   Combine 1 cup all purpose flour, 1 cup whole wheat flour, salt and 2 tablespoons oil in a bowl. Work oil into flour until crumbly. Add enough hot water to bind dough.
2.   Make 1 inch round balls. Roll out into 3 inch rounds.
3.   Spread oil completely over surface area of rounds. Sprinkle lightly with flour.
4.   Fold rotis in half, spread oil on top part of rotis. Sprinkle with flour.
5.   Fold rotis in half again making a cone shaped roti.
6.   Roll out rotis to make 6 inch flat rounds.
7.   On a hot tawa cook roti lightly on one side for approximately 10 seconds. Turn roti over and cook for another 30 seconds. Turn roti over again and cook till roti puffs up, or is lightly browned.
8.   Remove roti from tawa and place on a flat plate. Spread some ghee or butter on hot roti. Repeat steps 7 and 8, till finished.

Serve hot roti with most of the curry dishes in this cookbook or enjoy roti with a sprinkle of brown sugar.

Plain Puri

Ingredients:

2 cups all purpose flour
1 teaspoon salt
2 tablespoons oil
1 – 2 cups warm water
3 – 4 cups oil for frying

Method:

1. In a bowl combine flour, salt and 2 tablespoons oil. Mix till flour is crumbly.
2. Bind dough with warm water to the consistency of a bread dough.
3. Take a handful of dough and roll out into one large round about ⅛ inch thick.
4. Cut dough in small round puris using a small glass or round cookie cutter.
5. Deep fry severel puris on medium heat in a wok or deep fryer.
6. Allow puris to puff up. Turn puris over. Cook until golden brown.
7. Remove puris from oil and place in a stainless steel colander.
8. Serve hot or cold.

Spicy Puri

Ingredients:

2 cups all purpose flour
2 teaspoons ginger/garlic masala
½ teaspoon green chillie masala
1 teaspoon red chillie powder
1 teaspoon turmeric powder
1 teaspoon salt
2 tablespoons oil
1 – 2 cups warm water
3 – 4 cups oil for frying

Method:

1. In a bowl combine flour, ginger/garlic masala, green chillie masala, red chillie powder, turmeric powder, salt and oil. Blend till mixture is crumbly. Bind dough with warm water to the consistency of a bread dough.
2. Take handfuls of dough and roll out into large rounds about ⅛ inch thick.
3. Using a round cookie cutter or glass cut out round puris.
4. Heat oil in a deep fryer or wok on medium heat.
5. Fry several puris in hot oil. The puris will puff up into round balls. Turn puris over. Cook until crispy golden brown.
6. Remove puris from oil and allow to cool in a stainless steel colander.

Serve spicy puris with Traditional chai (tea).

Flaky Jeera Puri

Ingredients:

2 cups all purpose flour
1 teaspoon salt
1 teaspoon crushed cumin
2 tablespoons oil
1 tablespoon sesame seeds
1 – 2 cups warm water
3 – 4 cups oil for frying

Method:

1.   Mix flour, salt, oil, crushed cumin and sesame seeds in a bowl till flour is crumbly.
2.   Bind dough with warm water to the consistency of a bread dough.
3.   Take handfuls of dough and roll out into large rounds about ⅛ inch thick.
4.   Spread oil completely over surface areas of rounds. Sprinkle lightly with flour.
5.   Roll pastry tightly like a Swiss roll. Cut into 1 inch wide sections.
6.   Roll out each of the sections to a 2 to 3 inch round puri.
7.   Heat oil in a deep fryer or wok on medium heat.
8.   Fry puris in hot oil turning occasionally. Remove when puris are crispy golden brown.
9.   Remove from oil. Allow to cool in a stainless steel colander.

Serve with Traditional chai (tea).

Foolecha

Ingredients:

4 cups all purpose flour
2 teaspoons crushed cumin
2 teaspoons salt
2 tablespoons fast active yeast
1 tablespoon sugar
4 tablespoons oil
2 – 3 cups warm water
3 – 4 cups oil for frying

Method:

1. In a bowl mix flour, crushed cumin, fast active yeast, sugar, salt and oil till flour mixture is crumbly.
2. Use only enough warm water to bind dough. Cover dough loosely with plastic food wrap. Put dough in a warm place. Allow dough to rise for 2 hours.
3. Take handfuls of dough and roll out into 8 – 10 inch rounds ¼ inch thick.
4. Cut dough with cookie cutter and set aside.
5. Heat oil in a deep fryer or wok on medium heat.
6. Fry in hot oil turning occasionally. Remove when foolechas are golden brown.
7. Place foolechas in a stainless steel colander. Serve hot or cold.

Foolechas are fun to make with children. They love watching the cookie cutter shaped dough come to life before their eyes!

Garlic Naan

Ingredients:

4 cups all purpose flour
2 teaspoons garlic masala
½ teaspoon green chillie masala
2 teaspoons crushed cumin
2 teaspoons salt
2 tablespoons fast active yeast
1 tablespoon sugar
4 tablespoons oil
2 – 3 cups warm water
3 – 4 cups oil for frying

Method:

1.   In a bowl combine flour, crushed cumin, garlic masala, green chillie masala, fast active yeast, sugar, salt and 4 tablespoons oil. Mix till crumbly.
2.   Use only enough warm water to bind dough. Cover dough loosely with plastic food wrap. Put dough in a warm place. Allow dough to rise for 2 hours.
3.   Make 2 inch round balls with dough. Roll into round shapes ¼ inch thick. Cook on a hot tawa, on medium heat.
4.   Place naan on tawa. Allow to cook lightly on one side for approximately 10 seconds. Turn naan over and cook till lightly browned. Turn naan over again, and cook till naan puffs up.
5.   Once naan is puffed up or thoroughly cooked on both sides, remove from tawa and place on a flat plate. Spread butter or ghee on naan immediately.
6.   Repeat steps 3 to 5 till all dough is used.

Baked Naan

Ingredients:

4 cups purpose flour
1 teaspoon baking powder
1 tablespoon fast active yeast
1 tablespoon sugar
1 teaspoon salt
¾ cup plain yogurt
1 egg beaten
2 tablespoons oil or melted ghee
1 cup warm milk
4 tablespoons chopped cilantro (optional)
3 tablespoons crushed cumin

Method:

1.   Blend together flour, baking powder, salt, sugar, fast active yeast and oil till flour is crumbly.
2.   Make a well in the center of mixture. Add plain yogurt, egg and milk. Work in all the ingredients. Knead dough well.
3.   Cover dough loosely with plastic food wrap. Put in a warm place. Allow to rise for about 2 hours.
4.   Take handfuls of dough and roll out to ¼ inch thick rounds. Place on a cookie sheet and bake in a preheated oven at 400°F for 10 to 12 minutes or till golden brown.
5.   Remove naan from cookie sheet. Spread butter lightly on top. Sprinkle immediately with crushed cumin and chopped cilantro.
6.   Cut naan into smaller segments and serve hot.

Ba's Poora (Spicy Crepes)

Ingredients:

½ cup chana flour
2 cups rice flour
2 teaspoons salt
½ teaspoon turmeric powder
1 teaspoon green chillie masala
3 cups water
¼ cup oil

Method:

1. In a large bowl mix together chana flour, rice flour, turmeric powder, green chillie masala, salt and water.
2. Allow mixture to sit for an hour in a cool place.
3. Heat a concave tawa or non-stick pan, on medium heat. Brush oil on tawa. Pour mixture, using a ladle, all around the edge of tawa.
4. Allow mixture to roll to the centre of tawa. Fill holes by smoothing out mixture or by adding more mixture to fill any open holes.
5. Cook poora till golden brown on one side. Flip poora over.
6. Brush oil around the outside edge of poora. Allow poora to cook for about one minute. Remove poora from tawa and place on a flat plate.
7. Continue steps 3 to 5 till mixture is used up.

Pooras are great with Traditional Chai (tea) or with any of the vegetable curries or daals.

Basmati Rice

Ingredients:

1 cup basmati rice
1 teaspoon salt
3 – 4 cups water
1 tablespoon ghee or butter
¼ cup water

Method:

1. Wash* basmati rice 3 times in warm water till water is clear.
2. In a large pot cook rice on medium heat with approximately 3 to 4 cups of water.
3. Add salt and stir well. Cook for 10 to 15 minutes or till rice is half cooked.
4. Drain rice in a colander. Set aside.
5. Coat bottom of the pot with ½ tablespoon ghee or butter. Add drained rice. Drop ½ tablespoon ghee or butter on top of rice.
6. Add ¼ cup of water. Cover and cook for 10 to 15 minutes on low heat or till rice is fully cooked.

* Basmati rice is a thin long grain rice. These grains should be washed 3 times in a bowl with warm water. The first wash will leave milky water which is drained off. After the third washing the water should be clear. This indicates the rice is clear of any white starch and therefore will not stick together when cooked.

Yellow Rice

Ingredients:

1 cup basmati rice
1 teaspoon salt
2 cups water
2 tablespoons ghee or butter
½ medium onion finely sliced
1 teaspoon cumin seeds
½ teaspoon turmeric powder
¼ cup water

Method:

1. Wash rice 3 times in water till water is clear.
2. In a pot cook rice on medium heat, with 2 cups water.
3. Add salt and turmeric powder. Stir and cook for 10 to 15 minutes or till rice is half cooked.
4. Drain rice in a colander. Set aside. In the same pot heat ghee or butter.
5. Add cumin seeds and onions. Sauté.
6. Add rice and stir. Add ¼ cup water and cover. Cook on low heat for 10 to 15 minutes or till rice is fully cooked.

Ghee

Ingredients:

1 lb salted or unsalted butter

Method:

1. Place butter in a saucepan on low heat.
2. Allow butter to melt and come to a rolling boil.
3. Do not stir. Continue boiling for 15 to 20 minutes or till froth reduces considerably and you can see a clear gold liquid.*
4. Remove pan from heat. Allow ghee to cool down.
5. Sieve ghee through thick layers of cheesecloth into a glass jar.
6. Store ghee in a cool dry place.

*It is important for the ghee to melt long enough to remove all milk solids so that it can be kept for a long time.

Masalas see page 74-76

Spicy Salad see page 66

Condiments
Masalas & Salads

Spicy Salad

Ingredients:

2 cups chopped iceberg lettuce
½ english cucumber julienned
½ small red onion sliced finely
3 medium carrots julienned
3 celery sticks julienned
¼ cup green onions chopped
¼ - ½ green chillie
3 cloves garlic
2½ teaspoons salt
¼ teaspoon red chillie powder
2 teaspoons crushed cumin
4 tablespoons extra virgin olive oil
6 tablespoons freshly squeezed lemon juice
3 tablespoons chopped parsley
3 tablespoons chopped cilantro

Method:

1. In a large salad bowl add iceberg lettuce, cucumber, carrots, celery and red onions.
2. Add green onions, parsley and cilantro.
3. Blend together extra virgin olive oil, freshly squeezed lemon juice, salt, red chillie powder, crushed cumin, finely chopped green chillies and grated garlic gloves.
4. Whisk vigorously and pour vinaigrette over salad. Toss just before serving.

Tangy Cucumber Salad

Ingredients:

1 english cucumber cut into 2" wedges
1 teaspoon salt
1 teaspoon crushed cumin
¼ teaspoon green chillie masala
2 tablespoons extra virgin olive oil
2 tablespoons white wine vinegar

Method:

1.	Place cucumber in a bowl.
2.	Blend together crushed cumin, green chillie masala, extra virgin olive oil, white wine vinegar and salt.
3.	Whisk vigorously and pour vinaigrette over cucumber. Toss.

Raita

Ingredients:

I cucumber grated
3 tablespoons crushed cumin
2 garlic cloves grated
¼ teaspoon salt
¼ teaspoon red chillie powder
¼ teaspoon mustard powder
¼ teaspoon turmeric powder
½ teaspoon salt
4 tablespoons sour cream
1 cup plain yogurt

Method:

1.   Put grated cucumber into bowl. Sprinkle with ¼ teaspoon salt. Stir.
2.   Place cucumber mixture in a cool place for 5 minutes.
3.   Take grated cucumber in both hands and squeeze excess water out.
4.   Place squeezed cucumber in a separate bowl. Add crushed cumin, grated garlic, ½ teaspoon salt, red chillie powder, mustard powder, turmeric powder, sour cream and yogurt. Stir well.
5.   Place raita in fridge. Serve cold.

Katchoomber

Ingredients:

½ english cucumber julienned
½ small red onion julienned
3 medium carrots julienned
3 celery sticks julienned
3 tablespoons extra virgin olive oil
2 tablespoons cider vinegar
2 teaspoons salt
¼ teaspoon red chillie powder
1 teaspoon crushed cumin
2 tablespoons chopped cilantro
1 tablespoon grated parmesan cheese

Method:

1. Place vegetables in a large salad bowl.
2. Blend together olive oil, cider vinegar, salt, red chillie powder and crushed cumin.
3. Whisk vinaigrette. Pour over salad. Toss just before serving.
4. Season with chopped cilantro and freshly grated parmesan cheese.

Tamarind Chutney

Ingredients:

2 tablespoons tamarind paste or 4 tablespoons tamarind sauce
2 tablespoons finely chopped onion
1 teaspoon garlic masala
1½ teaspoons red chillie powder
½ teaspoon turmeric powder
3 teaspoons crushed cumin
2 teaspoons salt
¼ cup freshly squeezed lemon juice
¼ cup water (add if using tamarind paste)
1 tablespoon chopped cilantro (optional)

Method:

1. In a bowl mix together tamarind paste, onions, garlic masala, red chillie powder, turmeric powder, crushed cumin, salt, freshly squeezed lemon juice and water.
2. Garnish with chopped cilantro.

Cilantro Chutney

Ingredients:

3 bunches cilantro or 3 cups cilantro
2 green chillies (Serrano or cayenne)
3 garlic cloves
½ teaspoon coarse salt
3 teaspoons cumin seeds
juice of one lemon
1 teaspoon salt

Method:

1. Wash and drain cilantro in a colander.
2. Process cilantro, green chillies, garlic cloves, cumin seeds and coarse salt in a chopper or food processor till chutney is a smooth paste. Chutney can be placed in small sealed containers and stored in the freezer for future use.
3. Stir in lemon juice and salt just before serving.

Fresh Tomato Chutney

Ingredients:

1 large tomato
1 tablespoon finely chopped onions
1 teaspoon garlic masala
¼ teaspoon green chillie masala
1 teaspoon crushed cumin
½ teaspoon turmeric powder
1 teaspoon salt
2 teaspoons white wine vinegar
1 tablespoon olive oil
1½ teaspoons brown sugar
2 tablespoons finely chopped cilantro
2 tablespoons finely chopped parsley
2 tablespoons chopped green onions

Method:

1. In a glass bowl mix together, finely chopped onions, tomatoes, cilantro, parsley and green onions.
2. Add garlic masala, green chillie masala, crushed cumin, turmeric powder, salt, brown sugar, white wine vinegar and olive oil.
3. Stir well and serve immediately.

Mango Pickle

Ingredients:

2 – 3 green mangoes cubed
1½ teaspoons red chillie powder
1 teaspoon crushed fenugreek
1½ teaspoons turmeric powder
1½ teaspoons salt
2 tablespoons extra virgin olive oil

Method:

1. In a bowl mix together red chillie powder, crushed fenugreek, turmeric powder, salt and extra virgin olive oil.
2. Add mangoes to spice mixture in bowl. Stir well.
3. This pickle can be made ahead of time. Store in fridge.

Ginger/Garlic Masala

Ingredients:

1 cup freshly peeled garlic cloves
1 cup freshly peeled ginger
3 fresh green chillies (Serrano or cayenne)
¼ teaspoon coarse salt

Method:

1. Place garlic, ginger, green chillies and salt in a chopper or food processor. Blend till masala is a fine paste.
2. Masalas may be stored in the freezer. Fill small sealed containers or freezer bags with small amounts of masala. Seal and flatten bag, so that the masala is about ⅛ inch thick.
3. When you require masala, break off the amount you need and place the masala back in the freezer.

Ginger/garlic masala is used in majority of the dishes in this Cookbook as well as in the first and second cookbooks in this series.

Green Chillie Masala

Ingredients:

1 cup fresh green chillies (Serrano or cayenne)
¼ teaspoon coarse salt

Method:

1. Wash and drain green chillies.
2. Place whole chillies and salt in a chopper or food processor. Process till masala looks like a paste.
3. Masalas may be stored in the freezer. Fill sealed containers or freezer bags with small amounts of masala. Seal and flatten bag, so that masala is about ⅛ inch thick.
4. When you require masala, break off the amount you need and place masala back in the freezer.

Green Chillie masala is used in majority of the dishes in this Cookbook as well as in the first and second cookbooks in this series.

Garlic Masala

Ingredients:

1 cup fresh garlic cloves peeled
2 fresh green chillies (Serrano or Cayenne)
¼ teaspoon coarse salt

Method:

1.   Blend garlic, whole chillies and salt in a chopper or food processor, till masala looks like a paste.
2.   Masalas may be stored in the freezer. Fill freezer bags with small amounts of masala. Seal and flatten the bag, so that masala is about ⅛ inch thick. When you require masala, just break off the amount you need and place masala back in the freezer.

Garlic masala is used in a few of the recipes in this Cookbook as well as in the first and second cookbooks in this series.

Desserts & Chai (teas)

Seero

Ingredients:

1 cup cream of wheat
6 tablespoons ghee
4 tablespoons brown sugar
¼ cup raisins
¼ cup chopped almonds
1 cup water
1 cup milk
1 teaspoon ground cardamom

Method:

1. In a saucepan heat ghee on medium heat. Add cream of wheat and stir continuously until golden brown.
2. Add water and milk. Stir well.
3. Cover and allow to cook on low heat for 10 to 15 minutes, stirring occasionally.
4. Add brown sugar, raisins, almonds and ground cardamom. Stir well.
5. Cook for 10 to 15 minutes. Stir frequently to avoid sticking.

Cool Melon Dessert

Ingredients:

½ seedless watermelon
½ cantaloupe
½ honeydew melon
1 cup green seedless grapes
1 cup red seedless grapes
4 – 6 tablespoons honey
juice of half a lemon
4 tablespoons finely chopped mint

Method:

1.　　Remove seeds from cantaloupe and honeydew melons.
2.　　Using a melon baller, scoop out round balls of watermelon, cantaloupe and honeydew melons. Place in a large dessert bowl.
3.　　Add green and red grapes.
4.　　In a separate bowl mix together honey, lemon juice and mint.
5.　　Pour mixture over fruit. Toss.
6.　　Cover and place in fridge. Serve cold.

Barfi

Ingredients:

2 cups powdered milk
1 cup sugar
½ cup half and half cream
½ teaspoon saffron
1 teaspoon ground cardamom
½ teaspoon ground nutmeg
1 tablespoon crushed pistachios
1 tablespoon crushed almonds

Method:

1.   In a pan mix together sugar and half and half cream.
2.   Allow mixture to come to a rolling boil on medium heat.
3.   Remove from stove. Add powdered milk immediately. Stir well.
4.   Add cardamom and nutmeg. Stir well. Continue to stir until mixture is cool enough to handle.
5.   Line a 9" baking pan with wax paper. Spread mixture evenly in pan. Garnish with pistachios and almonds.
6.   Allow to cool for approximately 1 to 2 hours.
7.   Cut into squares and store in a sealed container in the fridge.

Coconut Squares see page 81

Iced Chai see page 88

Coconut Squares

Ingredients:

2 cups powdered milk
2 cups sugar
½ cup water
2½ cups finely shredded unsweetened coconut
1 tablespoon melted chocolate
1 drop red food coloring

Method:

1.   In a pot heat sugar and water, on medium heat, stirring regularly. Allow mixture to come to a rolling boil.
2.   Remove pan from stove. Add unsweetened shredded coconut and powdered milk. Stir well.
3.   Divide mixture into 3 equal portions.
4.   Line 9" cake pan with wax paper. Place first portion of the dough in a pan and spread evenly.
5.   Add red food coloring to second portion of the dough and mix thoroughly, till mixture turns a pinkish color.
6.   Place pink mixture over top of first layer. Spread evenly.
7.   Melt unsweetened chocolate in a glass bowl in the microwave. Add melted chocolate to the last portion of the dough. Mix thoroughly.
8.   Place chocolate dough mixture over pink layer. Spread evenly.
9.   Allow coconut squares to cool for 1 to 2 hours, then cut into 1" squares. Place coconut squares in a sealed container and store in the refrigerator.

Googra

Pastry

Ingredients:

2 cups all purpose flour
4 tablespoons oil
1 - 2 cups warm water

Method:

1.   Blend together flour and oil till crumbly.
2.   Add enough water to bind dough. Set aside.

Googra cont.

Mixture, Filling and Frying

Ingredients:

1 cup cream of wheat
½ cup sugar
4 tablespoons ghee or butter
1 teaspoon ground cardamom
½ cup unsweetened shredded coconut
¼ cup raisins

Method:

1. In a pan melt ghee on medium heat. Add cream of wheat and stir continuously until golden brown.
2. Remove from stove. Stir in ground cardamom, sugar, shredded coconut and raisins. Set filling aside.
3. Make Googra Pastry (page 82).
4. Take ¼ inch round balls of dough. Roll out to 2 inch rounds, with a rolling pin or a velan.
5. Take one tablespoon of filling. Place in the center.
6. Fold pastry together locking in filling. Pinch edges so that googra looks like a half moon shape. Repeat steps 5 and 6 until dough is used up.
7. Fry googras in wok or fryer till googras are crispy golden brown. Allow googras to cool in a stainless steel colander.
8. Store in a sealed container.

Sev

Ingredients:

1 cup very thin pasta - broken
6 tablespoons ghee
4 tablespoons brown sugar
¼ cup raisins
¼ cup chopped almonds
2 cups water
1 teaspoon ground cardamom

Method:

1. Heat ghee in a saucepan on medium heat. Add pasta and stir continuously until golden brown.
2. Add water and stir. Cover and allow to cook for 10 to 15 minutes, stirring occasionally.
3. Add brown sugar, raisins, chopped almonds and cardamom. Stir well.
4. Cook for a further 15 to 20 minutes on low heat, stirring frequently to avoid sticking.

Kharkharya

Ingredients:

4 cups all purpose flour
1 teaspoon salt
4 tablespoons ghee
½ cup sesame seeds
3 – 4 cups oil for frying

Syrup:

1 cup sugar
2/3 cup water
1 tablespoon milk

Method:

1.   In a pan heat water and sugar on medium heat. Allow syrup to come to a boil. Add milk. Stir.
2.   Remove from stove and set aside. Allow syrup to cool until warm to the touch.
3.   Mix flour, salt and ghee in a bowl till flour is crumbly.
4.   Bind dough with syrup. Make dough the consistency of a bread dough.
5.   Add sesame seeds and work into dough.
6.   Make 1 inch round balls. Roll out with velan into thin 6 inch rounds.
7.   Fry kharkharya in hot oil till pastry is crispy golden brown. Serve warm or cold.
8.   Store in sealed containers when cooled.

Sakar Pada

Ingredients:

4 cups all purpose flour
1 teaspoon salt
4 tablespoons ghee
3 – 4 cups oil for frying

Syrup:

1 cup sugar
2/3 cup water
1 tablespoon milk

Method:

1. In a pan heat water and sugar on medium heat. Allow syrup to come to a boil. Add milk. Stir.
2. Remove from stove and set aside. Allow syrup to cool until warm to the touch.
3. Mix flour, salt and ghee in a bowl till flour is crumbly.
4. Bind dough with syrup. Make dough the consistency of a bread dough.
5. Take handfuls of dough and roll out into 8 – 10 inch rounds and ¼ inch thick.
6. Using a pizza cutter cut pastry into 1 inch x 1 inch squares or diamond shapes.
7. Fry Sakar Padas in hot oil till they are crispy golden brown. Serve when cooled.
8. Store in a sealed container when cooled.

Traditional Chai (Tea)

Ingredients:

2 cups water
2 thin slices fresh ginger
2 tea bags
½ teaspoon chai masala
1 cup milk
sugar to taste

Method:

1.   Heat water in a pot over medium heat. Add tea bags, ginger and chai masala.
2.   Bring to a boil. Add 1 cup of milk.
3.   Allow mixture to come to a boil. Remove from heat. Remove tea bags and serve chai immediately.
4.   Add sugar to taste.

Iced Chai

Ingredients:

¼ teaspoon chai masala
3 thin slices fresh ginger
1 tea bag
1 tablespoon freshly squeezed lemon juice
1 tablespoon sugar
½ cup water
2 cups ice
lemon slices
mint leaves

Method:

1. Heat water in pot over medium heat. Add chai masala, ginger and tea.
2. Allow mixture to come to a boil. Add lemon juice and sugar. Stir.
3. Remove from stove and cool in the refrigerator.
4. Once cooled, place chai mixture and ice in a blender or liquidizer till ice is finely crushed.

This is a great drink on hot summer days. Use regular or decaffeinated black or green tea.

Chai Latte

Serves two

Ingredients:

1½ cups milk or steamed milk
⅛ teaspoon chai masala
pinch of cinnamon powder
1 – 2 teaspoons sugar
whipped cream
1 mint leaf (optional)

Method:

1. In a pot combine milk, chai masala and cinnamon. Heat on medium heat.
2. Bring to a boil. Pour into mugs immediately.
3. Top with whipped cream. Sprinkle with cinnamon powder.
4. Garnish with a mint leaf.

Mango Raas

Ingredients:

6 – 8 ripe mangoes peeled and cut into chunks
1 teaspoon ground cumin
½ teaspoon ground white pepper
½ teaspoon ground ginger
ghee or butter (optional)

Method:

1.   Place mango chunks in a blender and liquidize. Sieve pulp.
2.   Add cumin, white pepper and ginger.
3.   Serve in a bowl with a teaspoon of ghee or butter.

This is a great dessert or can be enjoyed with plain puri.

Chaas (Lussi)

Ingredients:

1 litre buttermilk
1 cup water
½ teaspoon ginger/garlic masala
¼ teaspoon green chillie masala
1 teaspoon crushed cumin
1 teaspoon salt

Method:

1. In a bowl whisk together buttermilk, water, ginger/garlic masala, green chillie masala, crushed cumin and salt.
2. Transfer chaas into glass jug. Store in the refridgerator.
3. Stir well before serving.

Chaas is a great drink on hot days and is also excellent served with any of the rice dishes.

Notes

Measurements Charts, Meal Suggestions & Glossary

Measurement Conversion Chart

Temperature	
Celsius - °C	Fahrenheit - °F
150°C	300°F
175°C	350°F
190°C	375°F
205°C	400°F
220°C	425°F

Measurement Conversion Chart

Weight	
Metric	**Imperial**
250 g	½ 1b
454 g	1 lb
1 kg	2.2 lb
1.5 kg	3.3 lb
2.2 kg	4.8 lb

Measurement Conversion Chart

Volume	
Metric	**Imperial**
1.25 ml	¼ teaspoon
2.5 ml	½ teaspoon
5 ml	1 teaspoon
15 ml	1 tablespoon
62.5 ml	¼ cup
125 ml	½ cup
250 ml	1 cup

Meal Suggestions

MEAL - I	
Bhajyas (Pakoras)	17
Aloo Gobi (Cauliflower Potato Curry)	30
Raita	68
Kadhee	48
Basmati Rice	62
Barfi	80
Traditional Chai (Tea)	87

MEAL – II	
Moothya (Spicy Patties)	12
Paneer Bhaji	28
Chana Masala	49
Flaky Roti (Chapatti)	54
Fresh Tomato Chutney	72
Seero	78
Traditional Chai (Tea)	87

MEAL – III	
Bhakro	40
Okra Curry	34
Plain Puri	55
Chaas (Lussi)	91
Traditional Chai (Tea)	87

Meal Suggestions

MEAL - IV	
Spinach Curry	31
Karela	32
Basmati Rice	62
Kadhee	48
Raita	68
Flaky Roti (Chapatti)	54
Coconut Squares	81
Traditional Chai (Tea)	87

MEAL – V	
Bhajyas (Pakoras)	17
Aloo Gobi (Cauliflower Potato Curry)	30
Raveya (Stuffed Eggplant)	35
Plain Puri	55
Mango Pickle	73
Mango Raas	90

MEAL - VI	
Paneer Bhaji	28
Chana Masala	49
Yellow Rice	63
Chaas (Lussi)	91
Raita	68
Garlic Naan	59

Meal Suggestions

MEAL – VII	
Vegetable Stir Fry	38
Tangy Mung Bean Curry	46
Basmati Rice	62
Baked Naan	60
Tangy Cucumber Salad	67
Cool Melon Dessert	79
Traditional Chai (Tea)	87

MEAL - VIII	
Vadas	16
Chevtee Daal	42
Okra Curry	34
Flaky Roti (Chapatti)	54
Spicy Salad	66
Bharfi	80
Traditional Chai (Tea)	87

MEAL – IX	
Samosas	18
Vegetable Pilaf	36
Raita	68
Tamarind Chutney	70
Cool Melon Dessert	79
Traditional Chai (Tea)	87

Meal Suggestions

MEAL – X	
Curried Bean Medley	47
Eggplant Potato Curry	33
Katchoomber	69
Yellow Rice	63
Bharfi	80
Traditional Chai (Tea)	87

MEAL – XI	
3 Bean Vadhu (Sprouted Bean Curry)	43
Aloo Gobi (Cauliflower Potato Curry)	30
Foolecha	58
Mango Pickle	73
Cool Melon Dessert	79
Traditional Chai (Tea)	87

Glossary

All spices, spice blends and cookware needed for Indian cooking mentioned in this glossary are available at Daksha's Gourmet Spices or www.spicesgourmet.com

Ajwan seeds	marjoram seeds
Aloo	potato
Barfi	sweet fudge made with cream and sugar
Basmati rice	thin long grained rice
Bhajyas	appetizers made with chana flour and chopped vegetables
Black mustard seeds	seeds of mustard plant
Brine	salt water
Cardamom	green pods with aromatic black seeds
Cassia sticks	outer bark of cinnamon tree
Chaas	spicy drink made from yogurt or buttermilk
Chai	tea
Chai masala	spice to make chai
Chana flour	chick pea flour
Chapatti	thin flat Indian bread
Chevtee	mixture of daals
Chop	cut into small pieces
Chutney	blended condiment made with vegetables or fruit and spices
Cilantro	plant grown from coriander seeds also know as thana
Cumin	also known as jeeroo, commonly used in Indian dishes
Daal	husked, split beans
Dice	cut into small cubes
Dokra	spicy steamed lentil cake
Fenugreek	bitter brown seeds also known as methi
Foolecha	small, round fried bread made with spices, flour and yeast
Garam masala	mixture of many warm spices blended together

Glossary

Garnish	to decorate and flavor a dish using spices or herbs
Ghee	clarified butter
Gobi	cauliflower
Googra	an enclosed pastry filled with sweet filling
Jeeroo	cumin
Kadhee	sauce made from buttermilk and spices
Karela	bitter melon
Katchoomber	salad
Kharkharya	crispy
Knead	act of pressing, folding and stretching dough
Limeree	curry leaves
Lussi	cold drink made with yogurt or buttermilk
Masala	mixture
Moothya	shaped by hand e.g. round patties
Naan	leavened flat bread
Okra	vegetable also known as bhinda
Pakoras	see bhajyas
Paneer	type of cheese added to curries
Patarya	spicy spinach rolls
Paturi	spicy rolls made of chana flour and yogurt
Pilaf	cooked rice with vegetables
Poora	spicy crepe
Puri	crispy deep fried round bread
Raita	cucumber condiment made with yogurt
Raveya	stuffed eggplant
Red chillie powder	made from hot cayenne peppers which are dried and crushed

Glossary

Roti	flat bread also known as chapatti
Sakar pada	diamond shaped
Samosa	triangular shaped pastry filled with spicy vegetable curry
Sauté	fry foods quickly in pan
Seero	sweet dessert made from semolina
Semolina	wheat germ
Serrano	type of chillie
Sev	sweet dessert made from pasta
Tamarind	acidic fruit that grows in a pod
Tawa	traditional Indian pan made specially to make roti, naan or pooras
Thana	coriander
Toower	a type of bean
Turmeric powder	yellow root which is dried and ground.
Urad	black mung bean
Vada	round crispy balls made with 3 types of flours and yogurt
Vadhu	sprouted beans
Velan	traditional Indian rolling pin used for making rotis, naan and puris

Index

Index

Index

Notes

Notes

Notes

Notes

Notes

www.**spicesgourmet**.com

Notes